Night at the
Musée d'Orsay

Also by Judy Wells

POETRY
Dear Phebe: The Dickinson Sisters Go West
The Glass Ship
I Dream of Circus Characters: A Berkeley Chronicle
Little Lulu Talks with Vincent Van Gogh
Call Home
Everything Irish
The Calling: 20th Century Women Artists
The Part-time Teacher
Been in Berkeley Too Long
with Carla Kandinsky, Ralph Dranow, Donna Duguay
Jane, Jane
Albuquerque Winter
I Have Berkeley

PROSE
The Berkeley Literary Women's Revolution:
Essays from Marsha's Salon, co-editor
with Marsha Hudson, Bridget Connelly
Doris Earnshaw, and Olivia Eielson

Night at the Musée d'Orsay

*Poems of Paris &
Other Great European Cities*

by

Judy Wells

REGENT PRESS
Berkeley, California

[paperback]
ISBN 10: 1-58790-640-6
ISBN 13: 978-1-58790-640-4

Library of Congress Catalog Number: 2022948051

"Starry Night over the Rhône" by Vincent van Gogh, 1888
(Nuit Étoilée sur le Rhône)
Musée d'Orsay, Paris
https://commons.wikimedia.org

Photo credit: Judy at Shakespeare and Company, Paris, 2005,
photo by Dale Jensen

Manufactured in the U.S.A.
REGENT PRESS
Berkeley, CA 94705
www.regentpress.net

DEDICATION

For my husband and traveling partner,
Dale Jensen
avant-garde poet

&

All who love European travel,
art, architecture, literature, and music,
especially my Comparative Literature sisters
from UC Berkeley

&

My early 1960s travel companions
from my Stanford-en-France VII group
especially Carole Magnus Grant
and my Stanford-in-Nantes group

Table of Contents

Foreword by Naomi Ruth Lowinsky

FRANCE

Night at the Musée d'Orsay / 3

I'd like to live in Paris / 4

On Seeing the Chagall Ceiling at the Paris Opera / 6

La Promenade: Marc Chagall Speaks / 8

The Swing / 10

The Matisse T-Shirt / 12

Asile (Asylum) / 14

Nantes, French Majors & Petits Beurres / 16

A la recherche du temps perdu / 18

Paris, c'est l'enfer / 20

The Traveling Priest / 22

Three French Haiku / 25

Balzac's Autobiography in Haiku / 26

Being Poets Together
in the Temple of Literature in Paris / 30

The Adventures of Lulu & Erik in France:
Lulu & Erik Visit Their Neighbor's Farm in the Dordogne / 35

ITALY

Roman Holiday / 39

Marys / 40

Fame / 41

La Bella Figura / 42

Orvieto / 45

Pentecost in Orvieto: Feast of La Polombella / 46

A Day in Assisi / 50

Ravenna / 53

Poet Jack Foley Says We're Not Writing for Eternity / 54

Procession in Kastelruth/Castelrotto / 56

AUSTRIA

We Skimmed the Cream off Austria / 61

The Traveling Mole / 64

White Gold / 66

Hundertwasser Went to Montessori School / 68

The Blue Dinghy: Hundertwasser Speaks
from the Future / 72

THE CZECH REPUBLIC

Romance in Český Krumlov / 75

Český Krumlov, May 22, 2013 / 76

The Bruegel Quartet / 78

Bugged by Kafka / 80

The Black Swan / 83

O Those Swiss / 84

SPAIN

Whatever Happened to the Golden Child
of "Las Meninas"? / 87

Pinturas Negras / 90

Homage to Catalonia / 93

Can a Catalan be Canonized?
Gaudí and La Sagrada Família / 95

Epilogue / 100

Acknowledgments / 101

About the Author / 103

Foreword

The first voice we hear in Judy Wells' *Night at the Musée d'Orsay* is that of a moth who confesses to spending the night in ecstasy on the painted "yellow blobs" of Van Gogh's stars, "reflected in a river." This humble, soulful art lover sets the tone for Wells' delightful collection of travel poems. Beauty awes her. She can swing from an ecstatic response to loveliness to an agonized response to suffering. Her contemplation of Matisse's *Icarus* on a T-shirt is broken by gunfire in Oakland, "and Black Icarus/ lies in a pool of/ brilliant red/ day/ after day/ after day." She moves us from laughter to tears.

Though Wells shed her Catholicism in adolescence, some of her most stirring poems are prayers. She prays to Chagall: "Let me sleep with blue roosters. Let me dance with red suns...." Chagall must have answered her prayers, because here we are, in Chagall's "La Promenade," hearing the artist tell us how he holds hands with his sweetie, "my Bella in her /pretty purple dress/ and guess what! She flies!" You've guessed it: to Wells, as to Chagall, art is a magical realm of bright colors and whimsy.

She prays to Valetudo, "Roman Goddess of good health/ you who calmed/ poor Vincent's mind..." so he could paint. Wells asks the goddess for more poems: "more yellow, blue and green/ moments of praise/ to this whirling world of wind/ trees, stone, and stars/ tourists and cars." Clearly the goddess has smiled upon her, for she gives us poems about painting, poets, cathedrals, culture, poems that move gracefully between French and English, and poems that reflect on a rich life, fully lived. Travel with Wells and you too will praise the "whirling world" and get your "*billets* to the universe."

NAOMI RUTH LOWINSKY,
author of *The Faust Woman Poems*
and *The Rabbi, the Goddess and Jung*

FRANCE

Night at the Musée d'Orsay

If the curators knew
I, a moth,
was in the Van Gogh room
at the Musée d'Orsay
in Paris,
they'd be shocked!
But what do they expect—
I love light
and I'm particularly
attracted to a painting
of stars—globs of light
reflected in a river.

I've sat on top of these yellow blobs
and survived somehow
though I can feel
the heat of these stars
right through the paint.
Light bulbs are cold by comparison
though I'm not singed by Van Gogh.
Somehow I'm transformed
and waves of ecstasy
wander through my wings.

I rest on Van Gogh's stars all night
and in the morning
I flit to a cottage
with a voluptuous garden
and settle on a deep blue iris.
The tourists think
I'm part of the painting.
I laugh.
I'm just a moth
with grand taste.

I'd Like to Live in Paris

I'd like to walk along the Seine
View Notre Dame de Paris
I'd like to live in the 5ème
Walk down the rue des Écoles
Sit at la Place de la Contrescarpe
and sip chocolate
Shoo away the pigeons
Hemingway stalked
for his stews as a poor man in Paris

I'd like to live in the 6ème
Walk in the Jardin du Luxembourg
Visit Gertrude Stein's place
Sit among her visitors
Picasso's great portrait of her on the wall
Alice with her brownies
about to serve us all

I'd like to live in the 16ème
or Passy as it was called
in the 19th century
Visit with Balzac in his house
where he hid from his creditors
Have him serve me a nightcap
of his famous coffee—
a thick brew made of ground beans
Then hear his stories *toute la nuit*
of Esther and Lucien de Rubempré
before I waltzed away

To stroll around Montmartre
with Salvador Dali

at dawn. Why not?
Or maybe I would join
Apollinaire and Marie Laurencin
wandering over bridges on the Seine
The sun rising slowly
on a cold, foggy day
My mind jazzed with Balzac's coffee
till I see Notre Dame de Paris

And bow my head

On Seeing the Chagall Ceiling at the Paris Opera

I once saw
dans un livre
Marc Chagall, *le peintre*,
standing on top of his creation—
the Paris Opera ceiling—
still laid out
on the floor
of his atelier.
His paint brush was as large
as a broom
and an explosion
of blue, red, and yellow
surrounded him,
a vast ocean of color
and he,
a small odysseus
with his picayune broom,
was exploring the universe.

Now, I stand
before this universe
in the Paris Opera
looking upward
picking out
the Eiffel Tower
lovers
ballet dancers
heads which look in both directions.
I pick out names
"L'Oiseau de Feu"

"Daphnis et Chloë"
and then
le petit nom
de "Chagall" lui-même
and I see again
le petit homme
from whose hands
and from whose heart
has sprung this ocean
of a ceiling
surrounded by gilded curlicues
and angels of another century.
The man is dead
and I am of this century,
the new millennium,
as Chagall is of the old
but let his colors
blaze through my life.

Come, Chagall,
surround me with blue.
Let me sleep with blue roosters.
Let me dance with red suns and moons,
yellow ballerinas.
Let me look in two directions at once
with my one good eye
and let me penetrate a heaven
of no rosy cherubs
but of vast blue angels.

La Promenade:
Marc Chagall Speaks

When I take a walk
with my sweetie, Bella,
after we have talked,
lounging on the lovely
red spread she has brought,
after we have sipped
from our one cup of wine,
sometimes, I feel so high
so drunk with love
for my Bella, my
sweet little dove, I
ply my magic! I
hold a little dove
in my right hand gently,
cup my fingers around its wings,
stand up, and with my left
hold hands with my Bella in her
pretty purple dress
and guess what! She flies!

Yes, my Bella flies
in her purple high heel shoes
and her almost transparent
purple dress. Yes!
It is then, I say, I'm inspired
to paint as I walk
with ma Belle, my kite,
my muse, my saint.
My how her energy
flies through my soul,

but I have my hands
full, in my right
my bird, with her own
fluttering soul,
in my left
ma Belle, with her own
fluttering soul,
and the moment comes
when I toss my struggling dove
into the air

And Bella drifts
gently down. It is then
I have to leave for town
very quickly to retrieve
my easel and my paints.
I leave Bella to gather
up the bread and the wine.
Later, she will find me in my
studio in ecstasy.
I have drunk from her body.
I have learned to fly
from a dove and a woman
and there she stands,
a red flowered tablecloth
in her hands
and begins to grow wings.

After Marc Chagall's *La promenade*, 1917-18

The Swing

I am standing
in front of a famous Renoir—
The Swing, in French, *La Balançoire*
Young woman in white dress
stands on a swing, seven
       blue bows adorn her dress
          from neck to hem
Oh how the light dapples down her dress—
       that Renoir touch
Those red apples on her cheeks
She looks away from her admirer
A man in light-dappled yellow hat
       away from me, another admirer

A voice, calling my name,
       awakes me from my Renoir reverie
Amidst the crowd, a former student
       "This is my favorite painting!
I came back through the rooms to see it again."
The crowd thickens around *La Balançoire*
       We step aside
"Did you hear about the concert?
       Last night.   At the winery.
A man committed suicide.
He climbed on a roof
       over the stage and jumped.
I was right up front.
         I saw everything."

She has a wild look in her eye
       I am horrified for her
"He was at the concert.

The music was very stirring, passionate."
        She waves her arms
"He acted on it.
I have to go back to my friend now.
We took off today to… " she hesitates
        I complete her thought
"to see something beautiful."
            "Yes," she says

I look back at Renoir's *La Balançoire*
Someone came unbalanced last night
All over the world
people are struggling to survive
        terrible floods, fires, cancer
            while a young man
swings out over center stage
        and lets go
            plummeting, plummeting
Stops a concert, traumatizes an audience
        Ends his life. Why?

I turn back to rooms
        filled with beautiful impressionist paintings
to hundreds of viewers
        struggling to understand
how that white snow can shimmer so
        how those green strokes can compose a bridge
how those blue bows can fascinate

Renoir, *La Balançoire*, 1876
Impressionism Exhibit, de Young, San Francisco, 2010
On loan from the Musée d'Orsay, Paris

The Matisse T-Shirt

I saw it in a catalogue
advertising chic artistic
       things to wear—
a Matisse *Jazz* t-shirt
100% cotton in true
       Matisse blue
Icarus falling soundlessly
       through space
so said the ad—

But when I pulled it
       from its package
and over my chest
all I could hear were
       sounds—
gunfire, brilliant shattered
       stars of yellow

One direct hit—
The red dot on Icarus' heart
His black body falling
       a crucifix
through Matisse's true blue
       jazz sky
and the sounds were so loud
       I knew
I could not wear this image
       blazed on my chest

Not here in Oakland
Not here in Berkeley
Not here in Richmond
where gunfire rings out
      in the night
cross-fire at dawn

and Black Icarus
lies in a pool of
      brilliant red
day
after day
after day

After Matisse's *Icarus,* from *Jazz,* Paris, 1947

Asile (Asylum)

O Valetudo!
Roman Goddess of good health
You who calmed
poor Vincent's mind
Calm mine!
You who helped Van Gogh
produce 100 drawings
150 paintings in a year
Help me produce
plus de poèmes—more poems
plus de paroles—more words
more yellow, blue and green
moments of praise
to this swirling world of wind
trees, stone, and stars
tourists and cars
art sellers
postcard sellers
of stamps, pottery, ice cream
billets, tickets, to *l'Asile de Saint Paul*
billets to *Les Bories*
billets to Roman ruins
billets to *musées*
billets to *toilettes*
billets to the universe

Let all the tickets swirl together
into a giant tunnel of plane trees
May they transform into birds
Billets to birds, to *oiseaux*   *Tickets to birds*
qui chantent l'espoir de l'univers   *who sing hope for the universe*
qui chantent l'amour   *who sing love*

14

qui ne chantent rien	*who sing nothing*
qui ne savent pas conduire	*who don't know how to drive*
mais tant pis—	*but no loss—*
Ils s'envolent	*They fly off*
pas de volant	*no steering wheel*
Ils s'envolent	*They fly off*
même dans ma tête	*even in my head*
et expriment	*and express*
mon désir d'aller là-bas	*my desire to go there*
où, comme dit Baudelaire,	*where, as Baudelaire says,*
il n'y a pas de billets	*there are no tickets*
mais tout n'est qu'ordre et beauté	*but all is order and beauty*
luxe, calme, et volupté	*luxury, peace, and sensuality*

Vincent Van Gogh resided in l'Asile de Saint Paul de Mausole in Saint Rémy de Provence from May 1889 to May 1890. The Roman ruin Glanum, with its Temple to Valetudo, is nearby.

Nantes, French Majors
& Petits Beurres

I'm washing dishes in Berkeley
in front of my kitchen window
      humming, singing—
When blossoms flowered 'mid the snows
      Upon a winter night
Was born the child, the Christmas Rose,
      The King of Love and Light.
And I slip back into Nantes, France
      50 years ago—1966
looking out my dormitory window
      on a cold winter night
Nantes, sweet smell of *biscuits* in the air
Nantes, home of *Le Petit Beurre*

Then, I'm at a Christmas feast
      chez Monsieur et Madame Weinstein
Monsieur, my Stanford professor
      accompanied us French majors
          to Nantes
      conducted literary discussions—
I still remember the mysteries of Kafka
      and his *Castle*
Monsieur never revealed his own past
      which I only learned years later
from his obit—Leo Weinstein, born in Germany
      came to America at age 15
escaped the Holocaust
      but returned to Germany
with the U.S. Army—
      He was sent behind enemy lines
to convince German citizens

to surrender.
He helped liberate Buchenwald
concentration camp
where his father died.

Madame Weinstein was always rolling in the tea cart
        to interrupt our intellectual discussions
with sugar, sugar, sugar
        more than in the Nantes *Petits Beurres*
we kept in our dorm rooms
        but in rich French pastries
We could eat them
We were young
They were filled with cream
We were filled with fervor
        trying to figure out Kafka
but we never knew Monsieur, our Professor
        was a German Jew
with a tragic and heroic past
        and perhaps he knew
more about Kafka than he cared to discuss
        with us
Americans abroad, still innocent
        still filled
                with sugar

For Leo Weinstein, 1921-2009

A la recherche du temps perdu

When I first went to France
37 years ago
where I learned to cross my 7's
The French were still talking
about *la Seconde Guerre Mondiale*,
            the Second World War.

Madame Paillet of Tours
parlait de la Résistance
            spoke of the Resistance
and how the American boys
from Stanford
with their blond crewcuts
reminded her of German soldiers.
The hatred was still there.

To us, 19 years old,
World War II was ancient history.
We were scarcely born. To her
Tours was freshly bombed,
freshly rebuilt.
La Résistance was the highlight
of her life
now confined to slicing *frites*.

Today, German tourists stroll
the streets of France
in great numbers
as if the war
had never happened.
Signs in hotels are in English and *Deutsch*
and small German children

have no inkling
not so very long ago
les Français et les Allemands
se détestaient.
       The French and the Germans
       hated each other.

C'est moi, it's I
who am backward now
living in a past
qui n'existe plus
       which no longer exists.
I have no children
to forget my past
so like the *madeleine*
soaked in tea
which gave rise to
Proust's whole past,

these German words
uttered softly
by these very pleasant German women
in this *très* French garden
of the *Hôtel des Grandes Écoles*
in Paris
evoke my past
but remembered by someone else—
Madame Paillet
Madame Paillet de Tours.

Paris, c'est l'enfer

"Paris, c'est l'enfer
et je peux le dire, moi,
parce que je suis parisien!"
"Paris is hell,"
said our taxi driver,
"and I can say that because I'm Parisian!"

And yet
the traffic was light
in the steady rain.
It was the Feast of the Ascension,
and Paris had emptied its hordes.
And no, our taxi driver
would not leave town too
but in a few weeks
he would go to Brittany
with his wife,
une bretonne.

Things have changed, I thought.
And I imagined the creamy white
rosy-cheeked Celtic wife
with this handsome dark-skinned
clean-cut North African man,
and I slid back into Nice
27 years ago
when the North African Arab men
hissed at me
as I walked down the streets,
Pssst! Pssst!
even though I turned around
and glared at them.

It was their game—
immigrant workers
without women
taunting a female tourist
in the miniest of skirts
and tiny turquoise halter top—
the only time in my life
I was ever bronze,
a skin which later peeled
off suddenly in England
to reveal my real Celtic
white and pink.

Today in Paris
dark-skinned North Africans
are still thrown up against walls
and asked for their *carte d'identité*
by *la Police*.
We saw it four years ago
dans le métro.
But other Arab sons
have grown to manhood
like this taxi driver,
assimilated and intermarried,
though the Bretons too are outsiders
with their own language.

I wonder now
what our taxi driver really meant
when he said,
"Paris, c'est l'enfer!"
Did he only mean the traffic?
Or did he mean
the steady, draining reign
of *racisme*?

The Traveling Priest

Our travel agent said
she didn't know
what we'd get
at the Hôtel Moderne
at Tours.
What we got
was Monsieur et Madame Saïd
on a very quiet street—
Victor Laloux.
Monsieur et Madame were not quiet.
He was a French Roberto Benigni,
a humorous trickster,
who offered you candy,
then took it away,
and Madame, a Lucille Ball,
who liked to toss down a few
with her diners at dinner.

I liked them, though,
this jolly couple,
who put to great shame
the French of my youth
who glared at me
when I said, *"Bonjour!"*
They were so jolly
we tiptoed away
our second night
to dine alone
without histrionics.

The morning we left
Monsieur et Madame showed us

a newspaper article
featuring them!
Two months ago
a traveling priest
arrived at the Hôtel Moderne à Tours.
Monsieur et Madame put him up,
and he probably dined
with their jolly personas,
Roberto Benigni and Lucille Ball.

He was a handsome priest
and young, gushed Madame
and she served him
the best of the house—
queue de boeuf.
"J'espère que ce n'est pas un aphrodisiaque,
parce que je suis seul ce soir," said the priest.
"I hope it's not an aphrodisiac,
because I'm alone this evening."

On the spot, Madame
had some *soupçons*—doubts—
surtout because the priest wore his cross upside down.
She even had more *soupçons*
when he asked for a separate bill for his wine
since *"L'Église,"* the Church, would not
reimburse for it.
Even so, Monsieur Saïd
would not call *la Police*, said Madame.

The next morning
the traveling priest said Mass
in a blaze of glory at St. Gatien,
then stole the collection box,
and left for Marseille

23

with Monsieur et Madame
left holding the bill
for his sumptuous meal
and his overnight stay.

Now the Saïds
can regale all their guests
with *l'histoire du faux prêtre*—
the tale of the fake priest—
one more in their repertoire of tricks,
but there's one detail
I left out.
Monsieur Saïd cannot drink.
He sucks mints for his stomach
and he's thin as a rail—
humor the flip side of pain.

Three French Haiku

Literary Travel

Large hiccoughs echo
over tumultuous seas—
Le Bateau Ivre!

Monet's Gifts

I painted water
lilies in the midst of war—
lightness in darkness

Storage Wars

Mouse chewed up Rousseau,
Proust, left turds behind. A real
deconstructionist.

Balzac's Autobiography* in Haiku

Young Balzac in His Writing Room

I hired a servant.
He's called Myself. He's not good
at sweeping. I weep.

*Balzac Receives His First
Authoritative Judgment of His Work*

"The author should do
anything he likes, but not
literature." *Merde!*

Balzac's Debts

To be in debt means
that you no longer belong
to yourself. I'm kept.

I owe my mother
50,000 francs and my
lover the same. *Merde!*

I wrote and printed
*The Art of Never Dining
at Home.* I eat well.

Comptes Mélancoliques:
my unpublished work of all
my debts, bound in black.

Balzac's Instant Aristocracy

My father escaped
peasantry. I call myself
"*de* Balzac." I rise!

*Laure de Berny, Former Lover,
Writes Honoré, 1830*

I burned your letters
and keep the ashes in an
urn. We shall be friends.

*Balzac's Critique of His Intended:
Mme. Hanska*

Without your mouth, your
forehead would be that of a
hydrocephalic.

Paris Life

i
Denial

Sleep: Two hours a night.
Orgies: Writing books. I am
        not a dissolute.

ii
Affirmation

Writing, I wear a
monk's robe. I am not a monk.
Who am I? You judge.

iii
Schemes

So, if I had been
a grocer, I would now be
a millionaire. *Merde!*

Balzac in 1840 Predicts
The Revolution of 1848

All "the youth of France
will explode like the boiler
of a steam-engine."

Big Fatty

My wine is Vouvray.
I possess 1500 pears.
I'm "*Gros Patapouf.*"

Mon Médecin Imaginaire

"Please, get my doctor,
Horace Bianchon," I
begged from my deathbed.

Honoré de Balzac, b. May 20, 1799 – d. August 18, 1850
Horace Bianchon is Balzac's physician character in *La Comédie Humaine*
*Information, translations adapted from Graham Robb's *Balzac*, 521 pages

Being Poets Together
in the Temple of Literature
in Paris

That's what Laurence Moréchand
called Shakespeare and Company bookstore
where she arranged a reading
for me and Dale, two American poets,
on Monday, May 28, 2001.
The world was not yet
split asunder by 9/11 but I was—
still in mourning for my mother
who had died six months ago in November.
Yet here I was in Paris
on a sweaty, hot evening standing
with my soon-to-be husband Dale
before a full audience, including
miraculously, three friends from Berkeley,
on the *premier étage* of the Temple of Literature—
88-year-old George Whitman's famed bookstore,
Shakespeare and Company.

When we introduce ourselves to Whitman,
he is either in his undies or a swimsuit—
I can't quite tell—
both appropriate for Paris' hot weather.
Laurence wants us to read inside
so up we troop the narrow stairway
lined with books and an occasional bench
laden with blankets, indicating a bookish traveler,
a "Tumbleweed," had stayed the night.
Laurence had found Whitman rather irascible

to work with, but he indeed had asked her
whether the Berkeley poets
wanted to stay the night upstairs
in the guest writers' room.
She declined for us saying,
"They'll probably want a shower, George."
Whitman's digs were not known
for their cleanliness and freedom from vermin.

We mistakenly troop up four flights,
then back down to the *premier étage*
where the reading is to take place
in a small floor-to-ceiling book-lined room
with a magnificent view of Notre Dame.
A young man hastily moves
his typewriter from the table
in front of the window,
but I have to depose the cat
from a chair on which it left
une petite goutte d'eau on the *siège*.
George Whitman appears in his undies again,
extracts a book from the shelf beside the table
and pulls out a pile of 100 franc notes
from the tome, saying, *"I trust him,
but I don't know about the rest of you!"*

Our host, Laurence Moréchand,
an elegant Parisian,
founder of *Femmes Artistes International,*
her magazine which highlighted
women artists from around the world
who had not received their due in mass media,
had miraculously interviewed me
several times for her review.
She looks perfect in her white frock,

artistic makeup and golden brown locks,
though even she looks a bit sweaty
as the heat rises in Shakespeare and Company.

The involved and curious straggle in:
Laurence's handsome boyfriend Dominique
with his video equipment,
A woman from Berkeley who can't stay,
A writer, Mark Lipman, who self-published
a novel and is going to the US to promote it,
A high school teacher at the American School,
My good friends Bridget, Hank, and Olivia
from Berkeley, all coincidentally in Paris,
A former student of Bridget's in Rhetoric,
A Muslim man, a young French woman,
two very young American girls, etc.
and Laurence's auburn-haired friend Pamela
in vibrant green and white striped sundress,
half-French, half-English
with a great throaty, hearty English voice
and a more subtle French one.
She seems so familiar
I finally remember she graced
a cover of *Femmes Artistes International,*
as "Pamina," a Parisian singer who does cabaret shows
with a glorious imitation of Yvette Guilbert
in her trademark long black gloves,
a favorite model of Toulouse-Lautrec.

As the temperature mounts in the hot sweaty room,
I read from my poetry book *Everything Irish,*
Dale from his poetry book *Twisted History.*
You could say our titles
comment on each other
but our styles are totally different.

I with a narrative style and story-telling voice,
Dale with an avant garde style, more surreal,
often using cut up techniques
à la William Burroughs and Brion Gysin.
Then we field questions like professional writers.
Dale is asked about the cut up process,
and he gives a very articulate,
almost academic explanation of its origins.
I am impressed!
I am asked why my work is poetry
if essentially narrative.
Hmm...I have to make up something!
"Condensation, rhythm, and my poems
actually do contain rhyme at times, but it's subtle
because the story travels through the rhyme."
The Muslim man asks about
"this sexual repression" I spoke of
in my poem, "Waking the Dead: Peig's Funeral."
It's fun to field that question!
I speak of Catholicism and sexual repression
versus robust peasant sexuality
when food was abundant in Ireland
and even Irish peasant wakes
once contained comic mimed fertility rituals.

It was a grand sweaty night
despite George Whitman
not trusting us
with his stash of French franc notes
in his book hiding place.
I did wonder
whether many other books contained money
the 88-year-old George had forgotten about.
Some weeks after we Berkeleyites
all returned from Paris

Bridget appeared on my doorstep
with a surprise.
She had snatched the elegant poster
which Laurence had printed for our reading
from the trash bin
and had it elegantly framed.
Today it has a place of honor
in Dale's and my living room
reminding us that we were once
honored to read our poems—
sponsored by *Femmes Artistes International*—
in the Temple of Literature,
the legendary Shakespeare and Company bookstore
in Paris, the city of light.

George Whitman, *b. Dec. 12, 1913, d. Dec. 14, 2011, age 98*

Sylvia Beach Whitman, *George Whitman's daughter, b. 1981, now runs Shakespeare and Company with David Delannet*

THE ADVENTURES OF LULU
AND ERIK
IN FRANCE

Lulu and Erik Visit Their Neighbor's Farm in the Dordogne

Lulu and Erik are invited to visit their next door neighbor's farm in the Dordogne. She is an artist. Although they have never been inside her house in Berkeley, she invites them to dinner 5,000 miles from home.

They drive up a twisty road into the hills above Saint-Céré at twilight and look for a barn with a blue door. The artist and her Wellington terrier await them at her ancient farmhouse painted with wonderful orange and blue shapes.

The artist gives them the grand tour of her *pré*, her newly cut meadow, where Shadow, who was a nasty little terror in Berkeley, frolics and transforms into sweet little "Miss Woo." The artist looks like a happy peasant woman in her blue smock. She tells them she's cleared 25 years of cow manure out of her barn, a huge pile of beer bottles nearby, and is renovating the stone pig sty into a guest house. She's installed water from town (her rights to the well were given up upon sale), electricity, and put in a bathroom. She would not live in France without a bathroom! She's painted her bedroom with clouds and sleeps in an old wooden boat bed with Miss Woo on a pillow at her feet.

She serves Lulu and Erik a hearty cauliflower soup, French bread, a huge omelette from her neighbor Constant's eggs, and a giant lettuce salad, also from his garden. Miss Woo partakes of the remains of the omelette in her plate by the fireplace. The artist finally brings out the pièce de résistance—a beautiful pear *gâteau* which the farm ants have ecstatically discovered. The artist brushes the ants out the window and serves it up with the local gossip.

"Everything you've heard about the French peasant is true," she says. Constant's father propositioned her in front of his wife. The older Frenchmen curse her and yell at her. Constant's brother is deranged and guards the sheep which graze in her meadow. "It's all here!" she says. "Constant's girlfriend won't move up to the farm and marry him because of the lecherous father." The artist used to give Constant her walnut crop every year in exchange for the food he brought her until she found out he made $3,000 from the crop and probably put up his big, modern, metal barn, which she hates, with her walnuts!

The wine flows, and the artist tells them about the famous American poet who has a house nearby. His first wife married him when she was 40, vivacious, and eccentric, and he was 20! She divorced her husband to marry the poet, and they bought the house in the Dordogne and put it in the poet's name. They eventually had an ugly divorce, and the wife lived there till she died, and then the poet inherited the farm. His second wife had a house on Maui, so the poet is now sitting pretty with two prime properties.

The famous American poet was very particular about his French, says the artist. He once messed up his future tense with a French woman and was so embarrassed he never wanted to see her again! The artist says her own French is execrable; she uses only the present and the *passé composé*, but she gets by. Lulu secretly sympathizes with the famous American poet. She can't remember the future tense either even though she lived in France twice.

The artist keeps farmer's hours so Lulu and Erik prepare to leave. Erik uses the artist's new bathroom. Then the artist and Miss Woo bid them adieu. As they drive back down the twisty road to Saint-Jean-Lespinasse and their hotel, Erik has a beatific look on his face. "That was a great meal," Lulu says. "Yes," he says. "It cured my constipation."

ITALY

Roman Holiday

Lady with circus
    striped suitcase, survivor of
cancer, is joyous!

Red brick high-rises.
    Red brick ancient Roman walls.
Time collapses here.

We are ripped off
    by Rome taxi driver. Even
Rick Steves can't help us.

Guides with microphones.
    Tourist-zombies all plugged in.
They are rendered mute.

Rome tourist guide sneers:
    "I know Rick Steves is your God.
He used to have my job."

Marys

Santa Maria Della Vittoria

Bernini blasted
    Teresa with orgasmic
bliss, even in stone.

Santa Maria in Trastevere

Mosaic Mary,
    your golden-jeweled mantle out-
shines even Jesus!

O Holy Mary,
    I am saturated with
your churches in Rome.

Delicate green rose
    on woman's neck in Roma.
Tattoo on brown skin.

Fifty years later
    Anita Ekburg's ghost still
roams Trevi Fountain.

Fame

I forgot about
   immortality in Rome—
thought only of food.

Guy who mops floor turns
   into head waiter after
he puts on white shirt.

His opening line:
   "Good food, bad service!" as he
ropes in customers.

Spoon Tartufo, dark
   chocolate ice cream with whipped cream
into mouth and swoon!

Pistachio nut
   cookie, o villain, you stole
my precious night's sleep!

Blue ice cream in Rome.
   Tourists will eat anything
that attracts their tongue.

La Bella Figura

Our last day in Roma—
We are staying at the Hotel Portoghesi
in the Via dei Portoghesi
right next to a small, but imposing Baroque
church, Sant' Antonio dei Portoghesi—
our little Portuguese corner in Roma.
We had noticed a flyer posted in the Chiesa
for a free organ concert that evening—
"Improvvisazioni sulle Sacre Scritture
e su temi dati."
"Improvisations on the Holy Scriptures
and on given themes."

We decide to go, expecting some familiar
solemn church music, Bach perhaps,
but what a surprise!
The organist, Giampaolo Di Rosa,
is a young, handsome, dark curly-haired
wizard in pink tie and stylish white jacket.
His performance is as contemporary
as his outfit, filling the Chiesa
with exhilarating modern music—
part rock, part jazz, part church.
I have no other word
to describe his improvisations
but "Baroque," exceptionally extravagant,
full of musical surprises,
as he works the organ pedals
with his feet, almost dancing at times.
If he were performing sacred music,
times have changed—
A rocker organist!

We leave the Chiesa exhilarated, energized
by Giampaulo Di Rosa's
"Improvs on the Holy Scriptures."

Outside the church
I want to congratulate the wizard
for his outstanding concert
but the rock God
in his pink tie and sparkling white jacket
has no time for me—
an older American tourist in her tee shirt,
khakis, and running shoes,
surrounded as he is by his admirers—
his much younger adoring fans.

I'm reminded
of a previous Italian voyage
we had taken to Bellagio on Lake Como,
a sparkling upscale tourist town
on that beautiful blue lake,
but also frequented by the Milanese
who liked to cut *la Bella Figura*
with their stylish Sunday outfits
from Milano's high fashion industry.
I remember Dale and I
promenading along the waterfront,
past tables of these fashionistas—
women in fancy, high-priced,
high-heeled Italian shoes
glancing disdainfully up and down my body,
then staring at my feet in my athletic shoes.
I held my head high,
looking as haughty as I could
for after all, I could walk
comfortably on these cobblestone streets,

even hike in the surrounding countryside,
while they would return home to Milano
with pinched toes and blisters,
sacrificing all for *la Bella Figura.*

Giampaolo Di Rosa is the titular organist and artistic director of the Portuguese National Church in Rome.

Orvieto

Bright clock on tower
    in blue-black night resembles
full moon, with numbers.

The morning bells of
    Orvieto ring out and
the fog disappears.

A gaggle of chubby
    Southern ladies in pastel hats
arrive with paint brushes.

Pentecost in Orvieto: Feast of La Palombella

I step into the Duomo
        the cathedral at Orvieto
to attend the 10 o'clock High Mass
        and am halted
                by an usher—
A procession files before me

A cadre of priests carrying tall candles
        a golden Bishop in his pointy hat
                then a procession of pairs
I am prepared for the men in dresses
        having been raised a Catholic
                and never thinking twice
                about this transvestism as a child

But the procession of pairs astonishes me
        Dark-haired, dark-eyed Italians
                beautifully Sunday-dressed
The older encircling the younger
        with an arm, protective, tender,
                a guardianship
                        male and female

I feel I am in a dream
        an initiation rite of old
                in a Temple of Mysteries
but I know what the mystery is
        as the beautiful pairs file before me
The adolescents are to be confirmed
        in their faith

by the Bishop
on this special day, not
just in Orvieto
but in all of Christendom
Pentecost

Fifty days after Easter, after
Christ has arisen—today
the Holy Ghost will descend
on his apostles
The dove will confer on them
tongues of fire
so they can go out
into the world and spread
the Gospel
in all languages
What better day than Pentecost
the feast of *La Palombella*
here in Orvieto
to confirm these adolescents
in their faith

I confess I have not professed
the Catholic faith in years
but the procession sends me
reeling back to my own adolescence
when I was a believer
when I studiously learned my catechism
so I could answer any question
the Bishop might ask me
at my confirmation

I would gain a new name
accept the sign of the Cross
on my forehead

the light slap on my face
The sitting in pews hoping
　　　　it was not I who had to
　　　　　　　answer a question by the Bishop

The procession of Italian pairs finally passes
　　　　Settled in my own pew
I witness the glorious High Mass
　　　　the shaking of the golden incense burner
　　　　　　　the holding of the jeweled Gospel book on high
But it is the music which soars
　　　　from the organ and polyphonic choir
　　　　　　　that takes me back to my teens
the glorious Latin
　　　　　　　of the sung Mass
　　　　the *Kyrie elésion*
　　　　　　　the *Gloria in excélsis Deo*
　　　　　　　the *Credo*

Why I can sing along
　　　　Latin, the sung tongue
　　　　　　　of my youth
My spirit soars
　　　　with the smell of pungent incense
　　　　　　　the pure voice of the priest
　　　　the pairs finally ascending
　　　　　　　the altar to the Bishop
The young ones
　　　　to receive their chrism
　　　　　　　their slap, their cheek kiss
　　　　their confirmation
still encircled by the arm of their guardian
　　　　(O guard them, dear sponsor, from
　　　　　　　the hands of wayward priests)

Then each young person
      speaks of their hopes and prayers
            to the congregation
      in Italian, sweet, earnest
O innocence before the fall
      into your full teenage years
            when you will forget
      all you have confirmed today
and enter the conflicts of adulthood
            but today you are pure
            I, too

And so I join the congregation
      after the Transubstantiation of the Mass
when bread and wine
      are transformed into the
            body and blood of Christ
O strange sacrifice
      O strange mystery
            O strange meal
and I partake of the bread
      a host given to me
which I place in my mouth
      as the priest says "*corpo di Cristo*"

I return to my seat
      not a hypocrite
but a renewed child
      happy to be with these Italians
            to whom I've said "*Pace*"
      and this is what I feel—
          "*pace*"—peace
      in the Duomo
          of Orvieto
            on Pentecost

A Day in Assisi

Train to Assisi

Huge cumulus clouds—
   full, white, puffy, turning dark
over Umbria.

Piazza Del Commune

I sip a birra
   picola on piazza—
become quite tipsy.

Pranzo

O pesto of pine
   nuts, basil, parmesan, and garlic—
You make me swoon!

Holy Grail in Assisi

A gaggle of nuns
   straggle up street in search of
the best gelato.

Basilica di San Francesco

Delicate pink sky
   surrounds grand Basilica.
Swallows swoop nearby.

On Viewing Giotto's Mural

St. Francis, like
   Allen Ginsberg, stripped naked
to start his new life.

Converts?

Italian bikers—
   local Hell's Angels in Church.
Will they be redeemed?

Performance Art, Via Santa Chiara

Man imitates Christ
   with sacred heart pinned to robe,
beckons from his niche.

Encounter

We meet Anglican
   Franciscan Friar on bus—
Only 150 in world.

He points out famous
   restaurant in Assisi—
McDonald's, of course.

Rain

Dark cloud over our
  Umbrian hill town brings rain.
Green fields below—glow!

Prayer

Saints Francis and Clare—
  Pray for me at the hour of
my death—later, please!

Blessing

Francis blesses us
  with blissful silence all night.
Morning bells bring peace.

Ravenna

2 a.m.
Drunk Italian men's
 voices echo off the walls
tutta la notte!

7 a.m.
Italian women's
 voices echo off the walls
of Via Rossi.

Are they bickering
 or just savoring early
morning good gossip?

Noon

Bells of Ravenna
 ring out, "Immaculate Mary,
my heart is on fire!"

I sing with them
 my childhood hymn
"*Ave, ave, ave, Maria!*
 Ave, ave, ave, Maria!"

Poet Jack Foley Says We're Not Writing for Eternity

but Renaissance artist Luca Signorelli
     painted the human body climbing into eternity
         in the Duomo in Orvieto
First as skeletons, then fully embodied
     as muscular young men and women
Nude, they push themselves out
     from a neutral white ground
as if they are coming out
     of hard ice, rather than earth
A few, still skeletons
     have yet to regrow their flesh
It's a hard labor, this rebirthing
     as two angels blast their horns above

Look at that beautiful, long-haired young man
     exerting himself like a mountain climber
         all but one leg out of the smooth white earth
That final push will pump
     his arm and shoulder muscles, chest muscles
         and those on that crossed front leg
His head and eyes are raised upward
     already contemplating
         an unseen God

Look at that woman, her breasts
     almost out of the "ice"
She has to be pulled through by a bending companion
     who grasps her joined wrists
Look at that man standing proudly
     hands on his hips
         reveling in his resurrected flesh

That damned Christian body
    that shamed Adam and Eve
        have no place in
Signorelli's glorification
    of nudity and physicality

We've had a rebirth here
    We've had a Renaissance
        We've had a peek at eternity
conceived by a tall, fair-haired painter
    dressed in elegant black garb and cap
        who painted himself in another fresco
Signorelli's eternity
    is inhabited by muscular, idealized models
        who must have held their difficult poses
        for hours
while the artist sketched them
    They rubbed their limbs with oil
        to soothe their aching bodies afterwards

In heaven, though, they are blessed
    No aching muscles
They gather in groups after their long climb
    slender, muscular beauties
Heads thrown back in ecstatic contemplation
    And we, too, tourists in this
        chapel in Orvieto
throw our heads back
    to gaze at eternity
to gaze at the inconceivable
    only to marvel
        at this very human flesh

Luca Signorelli's *Resurrection of the Flesh*, 1499 – 1503
Cappella Nuova or *San Brizio* Chapel in the Cathedral
(*Duomo*) of Orvieto.

Procession in Kastelruth/Castelrotto

for my mother

Funeral in Kastelruth
Funeral in Castelrotto
amongst a people who still celebrate
the old customs of Süd Tirol.
Men in Tyrolean hats with feathers
bear the standard: *Jesus/Farmer/Christ.*
The other old men fall in, in pairs.
Younger men in black
Tyrolean jackets, vests, and pants,
green asparagus branches in their hats,
bear the wooden coffin.
How heavy is the Christ/man inside?

His widow is majestic
held up by two adult daughters.
A tall woman, small face,
elegant brown braids
twisted round her head.
She wears a long, black silk dress,
with full puffy sleeves
brooch at the high neck,
a wedding dress in reverse.
Black, black, majestic
she follows the coffin,
face a mask of grief.

Women now in pairs fall in.
Everyone reciting prayers
in German.

Is the whole town here?
The little boys in their
purple and white altar boy outfits
stare at us tourists
as they enter St. Peter and Paul's.
They do not know
I too am here as a mourner
though I wear
a blue Gortex rain hat
running shoes
khakis and green vest.

I am here to mourn my mother.
I am here in black silks.
I am here with the widow
and her daughters.
I am with them
in the small cemetery
behind the church.
I am with them when the bells toll.
I am with them
when they throw
the last handfuls of dirt
on the newly dug grave.
I'll be there
when the red tulips sprout.
The pansies begin to grow.
I will sprinkle the flowers
with water from the little iron pot.
I will light candles on the grave
for 93 days.

Today is my mother's birthday.
Her funeral was six months ago.
I am here to commemorate my mother.

I will wrap black silk
around my soul.
I will wrap black silk
around my soul
so she'll know
for whom the bell tolls.

May 22, 2001

South Tyrol (German: Südtirol; Italian: Alto Adige; Ladin: Südtirol)
is a province in northern Italy. Until 1918 it was part of the Austro-
Hungarian empire, but this largely German-speaking territory was
occupied by Italy at the end of the war in November 1918 and was
annexed to Italy in 1919.

AUSTRIA

We Skimmed the Cream off Austria

We skimmed the cream off Austria
Ate the chocolate Sachertorte
Posed in the Tyrolean hats
Said *"Grüss Gott!"*
and tilted our mugs of beer
My spouse ate Wiener schnitzel
I ate creamy *spargel*
and all the while
we tried to suppress
dark thoughts of Hitler's Eagle's Nest
and concentration camps

We skimmed the cream off Austria
Climbed the stairs of Mozart's
"Geburtshaus" in Salzburg
Viewed the little genius's tiny violin
and saw a painting of his sister Nannerl
the other little prodigy
who toured the courts with Amadeus
While he went on to write "The Magic Flute"
her magic turned to ash
Father deemed she stay home
She married a widower with five kids
Proceeded to have three more—
only one survived—
Piano teacher became her lot
A woman's genius submerged

But we skimmed the cream off
Austrian culture

I thought about our former
Austrian-born Gubernator
Arnold Schwarzenegger
begetting four children with a Kennedy
and one more with her Nanny
Maria Shriver separated from the cad
Her journalism career on hold for several years
Now she speaks out for women
but she can't resurrect Mozart's sister
Nannerl

We skimmed the cream off
Austrian culture
Ate the chocolate Sachertorte
Learned Emperor Franz Josef's wife Sisi
loved pastries too
She married at age 16, hair down to her ankles
which took an entire day to wash
Gave birth to four children
then demanded her own apartment
in the Hofburg Palace
Did calisthenics on rings
she installed in her room
Traveled incessantly
and seemed clinically depressed
Her intelligence and ambition suppressed
by protocol and her role as beautiful Empress
in a gilded palace—
more like a cage than a fairy tale

But we skimmed the cream off
Austrian culture
Dodged the fake Mozarts
on the streets of Vienna
selling overpriced tickets to their gilded concerts

Haunted Stephansdom—
where a woman, a woman, mind you
in the great Gothic St. Stephen's Cathedral
put on a psychedelic light show
A Berkeley tie-dye light extravaganza
among the soaring arches
A rainbow of colors—
pinks, blues, oranges, and purples
and here and there—
a female saint or Mary
was highlighted with a subtle spotlight
Women honored in the patriarchal enclave

I suppose the artist Victoria Coeln
couldn't find the secular—
Mozart's sister Nannerl
in the Cathedral
nor the depressed Empress Sisi
but just the same—
She skimmed the cream off
Austrian culture
Found a way to honor women
in a temple of men
and whipped the cream up
till it was light

Chromotopia St. Stephan, Vienna, **2011-2014**
by Victoria Coeln, b. 1962, Vienna, Austria

The Traveling Mole

"La Traviata" outdoors
on a huge, full-color screen
at Vienna's Staatsoper square—
Free seats are set out for Viennese
and tourists who become
part of the opera!

It's almost a sing-along
when an audience tenor
begins Alfredo's solo on key
before the real star opens
his mouth on the screen.

And then there's the soprano—
the magnificent Violetta
dark-haired with porcelain skin
whose every pore
is magnified on the screen.

And look! That mole
that used to be on her bosom
has now migrated to her neck
during a scene with a passionate,
open-mouthed kiss with her lover.

I am so disappointed
we have to leave before Act III
as rain comes pouring down.
The Wieners and stalwarts
raise their umbrellas and sit in puddles
but we decide not to get drenched.

Still, I did want to see
where Violetta's mole migrated next.
On her lip above her voluptuous mouth?
Perhaps on her forehead
when she's quite near death?

Did the soprano who played her
view that dark mark as a good luck charm?
Or was she just playing games
with us, the peons
without hundreds of euros
for an inside seat?

No matter—
Her singing was thrilling.
Her acting superb.
I will never remember her name
but my memory still lingers
on her traveling mole.

White Gold

One holiday season
Dale and I saw Julia Vinograd
trudging up Telegraph Avenue.
We stopped to chat—poets to poet.
Sister Debbie Vinograd soon followed,
pulling a cartload of Julia's poetry books.
"Well, back to the salt mines," said Julia
and off she went to sell her wares.

———

Yesterday, I tasted
what *"back to the salt mines"* actually meant
to the 19th century women of Hallstatt,
quaint Austrian town on the edge
of a pristine lake,
famous back to pre-history
for its salt mines
high above the town on a cliff.

On an old sign, I read
that even pregnant Hallstatt women
made the 500 meter ascent to the mines
two times a day to bring down the "white gold"
lashed to wooden structures on their backs.
Their babies were often left behind in town
with a cloth doll "soaked in schnapps"—
emotionally, physically deformed children, the result.

———

6 a.m. this morning in Hallstatt,
I pull back the red curtains
in our chalet room.
The lake below is a perfect mirror
of white cumulous clouds and huge dark cliffs.
Mist rises from the lake—
ducks sail out from the boathouse,
leaving a shimmering V in their wake.

I wrap myself in a red blanket,
go out on the porch.
Thank God my task
is not to trudge to the salt mines today
and return in pain with my load of white gold,
but simply to sit on this porch
and experience
beauty, quiet, and calm
on the break of this ordinary day
in the universe.

Hundertwasser Went to
Montessori School

American travel guru Rick Steves
calls him "100 H2O"—
short for Hundertwasser.
He wasn't born with that name.
He was Friedrich Stowasser
born in Vienna, 1928.
You might not suspect this Austrian artist
had a dual identity—
Christian by his father,
who died a year after his birth,
Jewish by his mother.

Don't be too shocked if I tell you
his mother had him baptized in 1937,
and put him in the Hitler Youth Corps
from 1941 to 1944.
Wouldn't you also try to save
your child and yourself
from the fate of 69
of your Jewish relatives
sent to extermination camps
after your country was taken over
by Hitler in 1938?

I met 40-year-old Hundertwasser in 1968
in Berkeley at the Art Museum.
No, not in person,
but I'm sure he would have been a sensation
with his propensity to shed his clothes
and deliver proclamations

against rational architecture
in the nude.
Instead, I viewed his paintings.

45 years later,
before I traveled to Austria,
I pulled out my shiny, silver
Hundertwasser catalogue from '68
to inspect his art
His childlike figures
His brilliant colors
red, orange, yellow, green, blue, violet
His gold and silver glitter
His obsession with repetition
His spirals, eyes, windows, faces,
stylized aerial views of cities,
waterways, houses, parks, boats.

His surreal, colorful vision
fit right in with psychedelic
60's Berkeley though he took no drugs.
His travels influenced him—
Morocco, Tunisia, Tahiti, and Japan.
Paris and Venice where he had a studio/palazzo
on the island of Giudecca.
Did he feel at home on Giudecca
simply for the grand view of San Marco
or was he going "home" to his Jewish roots?

His Viennese friend and collector
Joachim Jean Aberbach writes:
"I never saw him without a satchel"
even at a Viennese coffee house late at night.
What did it contain?
A passport, foreign currencies,

toothbrush, toothpaste,
a miniature painting set
and color reproductions of his favorite paintings.
His hidden identity as a Jewish child
under Hitler had marked him for life—
He was always prepared to flee.

Hundertwasser owned four homes
in France, Venice, and two in Austria,
and eventually a farm in New Zealand,
though all but his largest paintings
were done on boats, trains, in hotels, or cafes.
He was the archetypal artist, wandering Jew.
Yet home and *haus* captured his imagination.
He and the architect Krawina
designed an apartment complex in Vienna
an eco house before its time—
with a patchwork quilt of a façade,
its once brilliant colors delineating space,
bright mosaics, striped pillars,
green foliage sprouting out of irregular windows,
roof top trees and onion domes.
"A golden onion tower on your own house
elevates the resident to the status of king!"
Hundertwasser spouted.
He challenged all linear construction,
boring boxes like
the touted
Le Corbusier apartments in France
which he despised.
No, give him Gaudí
in Barcelona
Give him the Watts Towers
by Simon Rodia in L.A.
Give him hand-fashioned

homes in Tunisia.
He wanted irrational beauty.
No straight lines anywhere.
Even floors should be curved.
The straight line is *"the only line*
that does not fit in with man
as being created in the likeness of God"
he proclaimed as *"Friedensreich"* Hundertwasser,
his first name now changed from Friedrich
to "Peaceful Realm."

Fittingly, he died traveling on a cruise ship
and was buried
on his farm in New Zealand
in the "Garden of the Happy Dead"
as he stipulated in a simple winding sheet,
60 centimeters down, only 2 feet,
with a tree planted over him—
his body recycled
like the bright mosaic pieces
used in his buildings—
his death now creating new life.

Friedensreich Hundertwasser
b. Dec. 15, 1928 - d. Feb. 19, 2000

The Blue Dinghy:
Hundertwasser Speaks
from the Future

It was a gothic window
    of a dinghy
I could see right through
     to the cobalt blue sea
      below
and there was an entire
     world there too
of gold glittery buildings

I remembered my stays
     in Venice
   many years ago
when I crossed the canal
      from Giudecca
to St. Mark's Square

That gold domed building
     is now under water
I can see the horses too
    four of them lying
      on their sides

I once believed Venice would last forever
    and I would too
Now I'm crossing to the other shore
     in my blue dinghy
to sing with the angels

After Hundertwasser's *Tender Dinghi,* **1982**

THE
CZECH
REPUBLIC

Romance in Český Krumlov

At my post at the window
     of our pension—
Across the Vltava River
     I contemplate a church steeple
like a Renaissance tower
       with windows
I imagine Rapunzel
     framed in one of them
letting her long hair down
     for her lover to crawl up
and into her

The sky constantly shifts
     behind the spire
       white clouds to heavy grey
I imagine Sisi
     Empress of the Habsburg Empire
taking one full day
     to wash her ankle-length hair
then perhaps
     letting it down
for Count Andrássy
       of Hungary
to wrap around his thighs

Sisi and the Count sigh
     for their illicit cause
their illicit child to be
     and the freedom Hungary will have
but not
     Sisi

Empress Elisabeth of Austria, b. 1837 – d. 1898, wife of Emperor Franz Josef. She helped bring about the dual monarchy of Austria-Hungary in 1867, though an affair with Count Andrássy is more legend than truth.

Český Krumlov, May 22, 2013

My mother's birthday—
      here's to you, Mom!
I'm in Český Krumlov
      in the Czech Republic
I hope you're in the Republic
        of Heaven
if such a state exists
      which I highly doubt
Nonetheless, you may now be
      a particle in the earth
        or a speck of dust
that has drifted
      into the Vltava River
outside my window
        sparkling slightly
on this overcast morning
      sun straining to break
        through the grey

I too now break through
      the grey of young old age
as the sun now
      penetrates my window seat
        and I write this poem
The church spire clock
      says 7:25—
I love knowing clock time
      but I don't know my lifetime
or the time of the universe
      or how old this plank floor
and dark wooden-beamed ceiling are
      I only know my own

69th birthday approaches slowly
  and 50 years ago
I was in a country called
    Czechoslovakia
under Communist rule
  hitchhiking
with a couple of Czech window washers—
  former lawyers
towing a beat up VW to Prague

Sometimes now, I still feel 19—
  the same age as the Taiwanese kids
in the train yesterday
  with their electronic devices
    orienting them
I still orient by instinct—
  often wrong, often right
    It's the way of the older generations
We know technology
  cannot answer how long we will live
no matter how many times
  we Google for an answer
I can only see the clock spire
  now at 7:30
silent, cross on top of spire
  pointing upward
when Heaven may well be
  right here
on earth

The Bruegel Quartet

This evening—
we saw the street brigade
        of Český Krumlov
A quartet of Bruegel-like people
        three men and a woman
dressed in ragged brown clothes
                and caps
A few without key teeth

One carried a white bucket of
        bones with bloody red meat still clinging
probably from the garbage can
        of a butcher's shop
O God, I thought
        Has it come to this?
They're going to gnaw on raw meat
                like animals?

Later, I remembered they were a quintet
                yesterday
A huge bloodhound on a leash
                in the lead
I hoped the offal
        was for this absent hound

The tattered group wound
        down the Vltava River
                on the cobblestone path
by our pristine pension
        I wondered where their lair was—
in what hidey hole
                they lay down to sleep

I remembered a dreadlocked hippie
        I saw yesterday
walking in the main square
           ranting to the air
    in an unknown language

Is it because I'm from Berkeley
        I notice the street people
among the hundreds of well-heeled tourists—
        European, American, Asian—
who descend on Český Krumlov each day
        to partake of a glorious Renaissance castle
a painted tower, a renovated rococo theater
        and an Old Town of intact baroque buildings—
façades and curlicues freshly repainted
           in grey, bright green and dark red hues?

There, I've almost forgotten them
        Perhaps you have too
The Bruegel people of Český Krumlov

Bugged By Kafka

5:45 a.m.—
I'm thinking about Kafka in Prague—
the key to his work: *Letter to Father*,
100 pages never sent
revealing how his father tyrannized him
all through his childhood,
teens, young adulthood.
Oldest son, expected to run
the family dry goods business
like his domineering, shouting father.
No, he would be a writer—
and a lawyer/bureaucrat
in a workers' accident insurance company
with days ending at 2 p.m.
so he could write.

Humiliated as worthless, no good,
never amount to much by his father.
No wonder Kafka's Gregor Samsa
woke up as a bug one morning.
Kafka's father viewed his son as
something to be smashed.
I always thought his alienation
stemmed from being a Jew
but no, probably not—
The family drama says it all.
Kafka was not a chip
off the old block.
More like a speck of sawdust
flicked from his father's shoulder.
His literary and theatre friends
were viewed as slime.

He could not even bring himself to marry—
that would make him too much
like his father, his equal,
such was his ingrained inferiority,
now adopted as his personality.

Yet, he wrote, wrote, wrote
through it all—
followed his vocation
often ensconced in a cottage
his sister Ottla rented for him,
of all places, in Prague's Castle
in the Golden Lane, #22.
Here he escaped Prague's noise
high above the town,
writing till midnight—
then descending to one thin-walled apartment
after another to sleep and wake
to his bureaucratic job
where he was amazingly successful
and often promoted.

T.B. would finally kill him.
He asked Max Brod to burn his works.
His friend published them instead,
and now we have our brooding Kafka's
face on postcards and marionettes
in Prague and a whole museum
dedicated to his life and literature
where you wander through
a dark labyrinth whose walls
are file cabinets marked with
the names of "Josef K" and "Gregor Samsa"
and old black telephones are hung on the walls
complete with German voice

on the line when you pick one up.
I don't know what the voice said—
something scary and bureaucratic perhaps
or maybe "You're about to turn
into a bug when you leave this museum"
or "Beware the rain. We're about
to have a flood," which Prague did
along with the rest of Middle Europe
a week after we left for home—
the Vltava, Danube, and Elbe
all overflowing their banks,
now settled down, I hope.

His character K never did get inside The Castle
but ironically Franz Kafka did—
wrote within its confines,
not in Habsburg aristocratic quarters
with gilded ornaments and curlicues,
but in silent splendor in a tiny cottage.
An unnoticed bug in a Castle
fortified against his father.

Franz Kafka, b. 1883 - d. 1924 (age 40)

The Black Swan

for Beatlick Joe Speer, 1948 – 2010
New Mexican poet, storyteller, omnivorous reader, traveler

I was wandering down the Vltava in Prague,
saw a tiny park, tall weeping willows, elegant swans,
a serape under a willow, and out popped Joe Speer.
He greeted me without surprise: *"My last day in Prague.*
Sorry we can't tip a pitcher of Pilsner tonight."
He sailed off on the back of a black swan toward the Charles Bridge.
I wandered to the Kafka Museum, a room lined with file cabinets
marked "Gregor Samsa," "Josef K," and "Joe Speer."
I peered within: one scrawled note: *"Meet me in Dublin.*
We'll read Molly Bloom's soliloquy and hoist a Guinness—Yes!"

O Those Swiss

Flight from Prague to Zurich—
Before we take off,
Swiss flight attendant
comes around with large basket
of Swiss milk chocolate candy bars.
"Yes, take as many as you want,"
he encourages us all
with a broad smile.

He's the good mother you never had,
the bad dentist,
the fairy godmother
with the magic wand
to soothe your airplane fears.
He comes around again
before we land
this time with huge chocolate croissants.

O those Swiss
know how to fly
even on a one hour junket
from Prague to Zurich.
O those Swiss know how to fly!
A chocolate high
will bring you down
safely.

SPAIN

Whatever Happened to the Golden Child of Las Meninas?

Whatever happened to the golden girl
of *Las Meninas*?
The beautiful child
The Infanta Margarita
that Velázquez painted
almost with a halo like Jesus
Whatever happened to Margarita?

As a young girl
she was betrothed
to Emperor Leopold I of Austria
No problem that he was both
her uncle and cousin
No problem that he was eleven
years her senior
At age 15, the golden girl
was sent from Madrid to Vienna
Married with two years
of pomp, ballet and opera
Fireworks exploding
far into the night

Within a few years
the golden girl had birthed four babies
Only one survived
She was no longer quite the golden child
whose full-skirted portraits
in pink dress, blue dress
were sent off to Vienna
before her departure from Spain

to keep the Emperor informed
of her appearance and upkeep

Whatever happened to the golden woman
now Empress of Austria
and the Holy Roman Empire?
She died at age 21—
worn out by endless births
and miscarriages, I suppose
That once radiant little girl in the white dress
with her golden locks
served by her maids
and a forthright dwarf
painted by the famous Velázquez
surrounded by light
almost a saint with her halo hair
was no more
I gasped when I read
she had died

Now her portraits fascinate
those enormous skirts
those stately poses
in 17th century Golden Age garb
In the 20th century
Picasso pondered this golden girl
Deconstructed her in his own style
Made her yellow, green, blue
and black and white—
Made Velázquez himself
enormous by her side
painting her parents

But I still remember the golden child
a girl like Jesus

so young, so innocent, almost holy
in an age of power
Whatever happened to the golden girl
of *Las Meninas*?
She's still there in the Prado
staring at me
in her hoop skirt
holding her pose
for millions of viewers
wishing perhaps she could drink from the cup
offered to her by her lady in waiting
wishing perhaps she could play
with her dog

Las Meninas by Diego Velázquez, 1656
The Prado, Madrid

Margarita Teresa of Spain
b. 1651 – d. 1673
Daughter of Philip IV of Spain and his 2nd wife, Mariana of Austria
Married 1666 to Emperor Leopold of Austria, Holy Roman Emperor

Pinturas Negras

Goya's "black paintings"—
Depression and gloom
glom onto me in this Prado room

Saturn Devouring His Son
Blood-rimmed torso
  a violent bite
      head already gone
Terror on the old man's face
  the fear and rage we feel as we age
Youth are taking over
  Devour them
      before they devour us
The theme of so much lit

And then the *Witches' Sabbath*
  The light dims in our consciousness
All rational thought
      all morality vanishes
We descend into the witches' hell
  to be initiated
      into their dark rites
by a huge devil goat
And in another "black painting"
  even our dog—our link to sanity
      is drowning

I emerge from the room
  drowning in darkness
      to confront again
not far away another Goya painting
The Family of Charles IV

All dressed in their absolute finery
    of silks and stockings and ribbons
Strip away Charles' white wig
    his blue and white sash
            and his buckled shoes
and watch him bite the head
    off his royal successor Ferdinand
His proud youthful son
            his flesh and blood
whom he now devours

Let his large wife Maria Luisa
    who bore fourteen children
and supposedly ruled in Charles' stead
    sit at the head of the Witches' Sabbath
A huge dark Inquisitional goat
    leading her flock of witches
            and warlocks
Only the faithful mastiff
    of the court is missing
Perhaps already drowned
    as Goya himself
            in dark shadow
peering from behind
    his gold and blue aristocrats
            royal children and teens

What restraint did it take
    to paint the shiny surface
        The Family of Charles IV
when beneath its sheen
    the deaf man Goya
knew the corruption of the royal family
    the dark of his own soul
            and the archetypal fears of all

death, usurpation
We will all be replaced
   by sparkling newcomers
and they too one day will become
   the aging Cronus/Saturn
         the Goat King or Queen
   the drowning dog

Francisco de Goya, 1746-1828
Goya's *Pinturas Negras,* 1819-1823, in The Prado, Madrid:
Saturno devorando a su hijo, (*Saturn Devouring His Son*)
Aquelarre/El Gran Cabrón, (*Witches Sabbath*)
Perro semihundido/El perro, (*The Drowning Dog*)
Goya's court painting:
La Família de Carlos IV, 1800-1801 (*The Family of Charles IV*)

Homage to Catalonia

We had been catapulted
to Catalonia— Barcelona—
and while wandering behind the Cathedral
we encountered a cultural crowd
sitting in a courtyard contemplating
the Catalan words of poets.

We commenced into the courtyard,
cautiously found two empty chairs
and listened to four Catalan poets
we could not understand.
This was not a catastrophe
as we comprehended the
emotional content and cacophony
of each Catalan poet whose
creations created our delight.

The first poet had a formal sound
with regular meter, a conservative approach,
despite his orange/pink pants.
The oldish poet had mellifluous music
in his poems, seemingly long lines
and solemn subject matter—death perhaps?
The woman poet had a conversational voice.
I snagged a few words from her confident delivery:
"feminism" and "Simone de Beauvoir."

The streetsy guy with shaved head
and pony tail was full of drama
and played with repetitive sound.
I heard "ch" "ch" "ch"
or was it "sh" "sh" "sh"

throughout one poem as the crowd cackled!
I wondered whether he was playing
with Catalan's "x" as in "*Eíxample*"
(the Modernista extension of Old Barcelona).
You don't say "example" as in English
though it's spelled nearly the same
but "Eye-shample"—"sh" "sh" "sh."

So yes, a Catalan poetry festival
we encountered through sheer coincidence
catapulted two American poets into a new language.
No, we could not sign up for an open reading
but we threw caution to the wind.
Said "*carrer*" instead of "*calle*"
for "street" (but not much more!)
and courageously embraced Catalonia!

Can a Catalan be Canonized?
Gaudí and La Sagrada Família

On an ordinary evening in 1926
Gaudí was walking to Sant Felip Neri Church
in Barcelona's Barri Gòtic to pray
when he was hit by a tram.
He was dressed in shabby suit
only a dried orange peel in his pocket.
A good Samaritan took him
to a pauper's hospital
where he received last rites
and died three days later, unrecognized
as Spain's most famous architect.

Gaudí may be beatified.
Next step, sainthood,
but what is his miracle?
La Sagrada Família itself?
Gaudí worked on its construction
for 43 years, dedicating the last
12 years of his life
solely to his sacred Temple.

2

What are these strange architectural words
which describe La Sagrada Família?
Hyperboloids, paraboloids,
helicoids, conoids? And the whopper—
hyperbolic paraboloids?
What discipline did I not study
in my youth that would have taught me

95

these terms?
Gaudí used all these forms
in his Temple which reaches
for eternity—
so I try to grasp these shapes.

Hyperboloids—the shape of the
Temple's huge skylights—I recognize
as the shape of today's nuclear
cooling towers and basketball hoops!
Gaudí says he took his inspiration
from nature. *A bone*, he says,
is a cylinder that ends in hyperboloids,
one inspiration for his Temple's columns.
Helicoids—easy enough—spiral!
His stairways to infinity are spiral
inside his Temple's huge bell towers,
a form found on a snail's shell.
Conoids—conical. Simple yet complex.
Paraboloids—oh my!
It's the shape between two fingers.
Gaudí says, *The paraboloid
is the father of all geometry*.
I cannot grasp this concept—
yet his bell towers are made
of intersections of *paraboloids*.
And his vaults use that whopper,
saddle-shaped *hyperbolic paraboloids*.

3

What I first saw, not geometry, but:
The Nativity Façade of the Temple—
a massive sand castle
in the rain, as if a giant

had dripped wet sand
down upon his huge creation,
yet up close in niches
were sacred figures,
and yes, there's Jesus, Mary, and Joseph
"La Sagrada Família."
I heard a guide say,
We should all pattern our families
after the Holy Family,
and I thought, Yes! Jesus!
One child policy!
Solve overpopulation!
Yet today we are all part
of la Sagrada Família,
saints and sinners
tourists and devout.

I enter La Sagrada Família
and find not a Basilica
but a sacred grove
whose soaring columns are tree trunks
opening to branches heavenward
and to great leaves.
Skylights defuse golden light
through these branches from above
and on either side of the grove
huge stained glass windows
color our world with blues and greens
to the East, reds and oranges to the West,
Christ's Nativity and Passion captured in light.
I am overwhelmed, awe struck
to have entered a structure
that evokes transcendence, God,
even when one is not a believer.
Is this Gaudí's miracle?

4

That woman with her selfie-stick,
videoing herself as she walks
through the Temple
does not experience it.
When she gets home
she will see her own videoed face
the one she sees in her mirror everyday.
Instead of soaring
she will fall into the pool
of her own solemn image.

Those teenage girls, posing giddily
in front of those huge, bronze *Pare Nostre* doors
with "*Give us this day our daily bread*"
in fifty languages raised on its surface
will see the miracle of their youth
on Facebook, but not Gaudí's
vision of infinity created
out of space, light, and stone.
They must come again
to really see his vision.

And so must I—
So much more to construct
for the Basilica—
the Glory Façade with its four bell towers
the Four Evangelists' Towers
the Our Lady Tower
and finally the huge Jesus Tower,
the pinnacle of the Temple.
Will I ever see again
La Sagrada Família
without the scaffolding

the huge cranes
the screeching of the workmen's tools
that compete with the Angelus
without the worker in his yellow hard hat
descending in the tubular
space age elevator,
a latter day Gaudí off to lunch?

5

I am 72 years old—
Projected finish of The Temple
10 more years—2026—
the 100th anniversary of Gaudí's death,
that fatal blow by the street car
that snatched the great architect
away from his sacred project.
That was no miracle.
But the miracle is
his project still lives
despite the Spanish Civil War
when Gaudí's workshop was destroyed.
His plaster models lay broken on the floor
but were salvaged and reconstructed
for future architects
to complete his plans.
St. Antoni Gaudí.
Try it out for sound.
Sant Antoni Gaudí.
A Catalan saint.
A world saint.
A universal saint.
A saint who sought infinity.

Epilogue:

If your structure rivals God's creation,
will there be a fatal flaw?
In 2010 the Spaniards bored a tunnel
for their high speed train
under La Sagrada Família.
Need I say more?

*"It is not a disappointment that I will not be able to finish the
temple. I will grow old, but others will come after me. What must
be always preserved is the spirit of the work; its life will depend on
the generations that transmit this spirit and bring it to life."*
Antoni Gaudí, b. 1852- d. 1926

1883
**Gaudí takes over as architect of the Expiatory Temple of the
Sagrada Família**

1936
**Spanish Civil War, destruction in the Church,
Gaudi's studio destroyed**

2010
**Pope Benedict XVI confers title of Basilica
on the Temple**

Acknowledgments

I would like to thank the editors of the publications in which these poems appeared, sometimes in slightly different form.

Awaa-te, 1995: "The Matisse T-Shirt"

Berkeley Daily Planet, 2008: "Night at the Musée d'Orsay," "I'd like to live in Paris"

Berkeley Times, v. 9, No. 19, August 15, 2019 (Poetry Edition): "A Day in Assisi"

Colere, Coe College, 2002: "Paris, c'est l'enfer"

Crazy Child Scribbler, #82, 2015: "The Traveling Mole"

Feile-Festa Literary Arts Journal, Spring 2011: "Poet Jack Foley Says We're Not Writing for Eternity"

I Dream of Circus Characters: A Berkeley Chronicle, poems by Judy Wells, Beatitude Press, 2010: "The Matisse T-Shirt"

Mo, Jo: The Anthology, John Roche, ed., Beatlick Press, 2014: "The Black Swan"

North Coast Literary Review, 2008: "On Seeing the Chagall Ceiling at the Paris Opera"

Poetry Expressed, v.1, Spring 2016: "The Swing" (and www. poetryexpressed.com Jan. 2016)

Rattlesnake 21, 2009: "Night at the Musée d'Orsay"

Reunion: Stanford-in-France VII, 2006: "A la recherche du temps perdu"

Stanford 50ᵗʰ Reunion Class Book, 2016: "Nantes, French Majors & Petits Beurres"

http://levurelitteraire.com/numero-4/ Nov. 2011: "The Matisse T-Shirt"

www.beatlick.com, 2016: "I'd like to live in Paris"

www.examiner.com/poetry-in-oakland/cherise-wyneken, Feb. 15, 2012: "The Swing"

www.sfpeaceandhope.com Issue #2, 2012: "Monet's Gifts"

I would also like to thank Mark Weiman of Regent Press in Berkeley for designing, typesetting, and publishing *Night at the Musée d'Orsay: Poems of Paris & Other Great European Cities*. It's been a pleasure working with him to create this beautiful book.

About the Author

JUDY WELLS is a fourth generation San Francisco Bay Area Californian. She received her B.A. in French from Stanford University and Ph.D. in Comparative Literature from UC Berkeley. She has twelve previous poetry books to her credit, including her exploration of her maternal Irish roots in her trilogy, *Everything Irish* and *Call Home* (Scarlet Tanager Books) and *The Glass Ship* (Sugartown Publishing). Her most recent collection, *Dear Phebe: The Dickinson Sisters Go West* (Sugartown), is a poetry/memoir about her paternal great-grandmother and her sisters, who came out to California in the early 1860s from Massachusetts to be pioneer schoolteachers. Judy's research revealed she is indeed a distant cousin of Emily Dickinson.

Judy has read her poetry in many venues—from the famed bookstore, Shakespeare & Co. in Paris to the famed, now closed Cody's Books on Telegraph Avenue in Berkeley. She has also been a featured reader in several Berkeley Poetry Festivals. Her poetry has appeared in *Veils, Halos, and Shackles: International Poetry on the Oppression and Empowerment of Women; Women Write Resistance; Berkeley Times; San Francisco Peace and Hope; California Quarterly; Marin Poetry Center Anthology; Stanford Alumni Magazine; Psychological Perspectives; Persimmon Tree; Timberline Review; Levure littéraire; Turning a Train of Thought Upside Down: An Anthology of Women's Poetry* and in many other journals.

She is also co-editor of *The Berkeley Literary Women's Revolution: Essays from Marsha's Salon*, McFarland, 2005, a chronicle of the founding of Women's Studies in the Comparative Literature Department at UC Berkeley in the 1970s. Her essays have appeared in *Travelers' Tales Ireland, The Borzoi College Reader, Value: Essays, Stories & Poems by Women of a Certain Age*, and *Not Dead Yet: Feminism, Passion and Women's Liberation*.

Judy taught writing and literature at various Bay Area colleges before a career as an Academic Counselor for adults in the School of Extended Education at Saint Mary's College of California, and as a faculty member of the Graduate Liberal Studies Program at Saint Mary's. She also taught writing at UC Berkeley Extension in a special Fall program for Cal freshmen. She is an active member of the San Francisco Bay Area Women's Poetry Salon, and lives with her husband, avant-garde poet Dale Jensen in Berkeley. www.judywellspoet.com

Judy at Shakespeare and Company, Paris, 2005,
photo by Dale Jensen